Collins English Readers

Amazing Performers

Level 3
CEF B1

D1245349

Text by
Jane Rollason

Series edited by
Fiona MacKenzie

Collins

HarperCollins Publishers
77–85 Fulham Palace Road
Hammersmith London W6 8JB

10 9 8 7 6 5 4 3 2 1

Original text
© The Amazing People Club Ltd

Adapted text
© HarperCollins Publishers Ltd 2014

ISBN: 978-0-00-754505-6

Cover image © Thomas Bethge/
Shutterstock

MIX
Paper from
responsible sources

FSC
www.fsc.org   **FSC™ C007454**

FSC™ is a non-profit international organisation established to promote the
responsible management of the world's forests. Products carrying the FSC
label are independently certified to assure consumers that they come from
forests that are managed to meet the social, economic and ecological needs
of present and future generations, and other controlled sources.

Find out more about HarperCollins and the environment at
www.harpercollins.co.uk/green

⋄ Contents ⋄

Introduction 4

Pablo Casals 7

Louis Armstrong 21

Frank Sinatra 35

Edith Piaf 49

Maria Callas 61

Elvis Presley 75

Glossary 88

◆ Introduction ◆

Collins Amazing People Readers are collections of short stories. Each book presents the life story of five or six people whose lives and achievements have made a difference to our world today. The stories are carefully graded to ensure that you, the reader, will both enjoy and benefit from your reading experience.

You can choose to enjoy the book from start to finish or to dip into your favourite story straight away. Each story is entirely independent.

After every story a short timeline brings together the most important events in each person's life into one short report. The timeline is a useful tool for revision purposes.

Words which are above the required reading level are underlined the first time they appear in each story. All underlined words are defined in the glossary at the back of the book. Levels 1 and 2 take their definitions from the *Collins COBUILD Essential English Dictionary* and levels 3 and 4 from the *Collins COBUILD Advanced English Dictionary*.

To support both teachers and learners, additional materials are available online at www.collinselt.com/readers.

The Amazing People Club®

Collins Amazing People Readers are adaptations of original texts published by The Amazing People Club. The Amazing People Club is an educational publishing house. It was founded in 2006 by educational psychologist and management leader Dr Charles Margerison and publishes books, eBooks, audio books, iBooks and video content, which bring readers 'face to face' with many of the world's most inspiring and influential characters from the fields of art, science, music, politics, medicine and business.

◆ The Grading Scheme ◆

The Collins COBUILD Grading Scheme has been created using the most up-to-date language usage information available today. Each level is guided by a brand new comprehensive grammar and vocabulary framework, ensuring that the series will perfectly match readers' abilities.

		CEF band	Pages	Word count	Headwords
Level 1	elementary	A2	64	5,000–8,000	approx. 700
Level 2	pre-intermediate	A2–B1	80	8,000–11,000	approx. 900
Level 3	intermediate	B1	96	11,000–15,000	approx. 1,100
Level 4	upper intermediate	B2	112	15,000–19,000	approx. 1,700

For more information on the Collins COBUILD Grading Scheme, including a full list of the grammar structures found at each level, go to www.collinselt.com/readers/gradingscheme.

Also available online: Make sure that you are reading at the right level by checking your level on our website (www.collinselt.com/readers/levelcheck).

Pablo Casals

◆ ◆ ◆

1876–1973

the Catalan cello-player

I had two loves in my life – music and Catalonia, the place where I was born. Music was always with me, but I had to leave Catalonia because of war. I was never able to return. So my life is a story of happiness and sadness.

◆ ◆ ◆

I was born on 29th December 1876 in El Vendrell in Catalonia into a <u>proud</u> Catalan family. Although my mother was born in Puerto Rico, her parents were Catalan too. Let me explain. Catalonia is the north-east region of Spain, with Barcelona as its regional capital. The Catalan people are very independent, and they have their own language and culture. Although they are part of Spain, many of them would like Catalonia to be an independent country.

My family was very musical, and music was always my first language. My father played and sang music in our local church, and he often took me with him. He gave me lessons, too, and by the age of four I could play the piano. Father was a good teacher. I gave my first public performance on the violin when I was six. It was not a completely happy experience, however, as a group of boys laughed at me because I played with my eyes closed.

Some travelling musicians visited El Vendrell one year, and they played some wonderful music. Among their instruments was a <u>cello</u>, which I had never heard before. Although I was only 11 I decided then that the cello was the instrument for me. Now I needed a cello teacher, so my mother took me to the Escola Municipal de Música in Barcelona, about 70 kilometres north of El Vendrell. I studied hard, and in my <u>free</u> time after school and at weekends, I searched the city's music shops for interesting music. I discovered a copy of 'Six Suites for <u>Solo</u> Cello' by J.S. Bach, which was like finding six bars of gold! Every day, I studied the music and played a little bit more, although I did not play Bach's Suites in public until 13 years later.

There was no television at that time, or even radio. If people wanted to hear music, they had to go to a concert hall or a café. I played in cafés every evening, sometimes popular music and sometimes classical, and it was a very important part of my musical education. I earned money, too, which I used to pay for my teaching.

Five years later, I completed my studies at the Escola Municipal in Barcelona, but I didn't know what kind of job I could get. I continued to play in cafés, and one day a man spoke to me. He told me he had enjoyed my playing very much, and then he introduced himself. He was Isaac Albéniz, a very famous pianist and composer at the time. As he was leaving the café, he gave me a note and told me to take it to the royal palace. The palace was the home of the Queen Maria Cristina, widow of King Alfonso and mother of the future king, who was then only eight years old.

I thought he was joking, but in fact I was invited to play for Queen Maria Cristina, and she loved my music. The letter also introduced me to Count Morphy, who took an interest in my education and taught me art, philosophy and maths. With help from the Queen and the Count, I was able to study <u>composition</u> at the Real Conservatorio de Música y Declamación. I played there with the Quartet Society. That was my first proper job as a musician.

♦ ◆ ♦

I loved playing at the palace, but I knew that I had to go abroad to have a successful career in music. I needed to meet

other musicians and <u>conductors</u>, and play with <u>orchestras</u> in different cities. I moved to Paris with my mother. We had very little money, but in 1895, I found a job playing in an orchestra in a <u>musical theatre</u>. I had to learn French quickly. Then an offer came from Barcelona, from the Gran Teatre del Liceu. They were looking for a cellist, and I was happy to return to my home city. I did not stay long, however. The following year I joined the Madrid Symphony Orchestra, and I played <u>solo</u> for Queen Maria Cristina.

I developed my own <u>style</u> of playing, which was unlike the style of most other cellists at that time. I tried to express my emotions through the cello. People seemed to like my new style, and I was becoming known outside Spain. I was invited to England, where I played a public concert in London and a private concert for Queen Victoria, at her summer palace on the Isle of Wight. I had invitations to play in Holland, the United States and South America. In 1904, I performed for Theodore Roosevelt, the President of the United States, at the White House in Washington DC.

While I was in America, I was asked to play the piano for an opera singer, called Susan Metcalfe. We soon fell in love, but we had very little time together. We were both performers, and our concerts took us to opposite sides of the world. Because there was no time for a private life together, our relationship sadly seemed to have no future.

Two years later, in 1906, I met a young Portuguese cellist and fell in love again. Her name was Guilhermina Suggia, and she became my student. We had six wonderful musical years together, but slowly our lives began to go separate ways. Not long after my relationship with Guilhermina ended, Susan Metcalfe appeared at my dressing-room door after a performance in Berlin one evening. Susan and I fell in love all over again, and this time we married.

It was 1914, and the First World War started in Europe. The German army were in France and there were terrible battles all over Europe. Susan and I left for the United States. As the war continued, Susan and I played many concerts together in the United States. We loved each other, but we had many arguments.

After the war, our work took us abroad again. I set up the Pablo Casals Orchestra in Barcelona in 1919, and in Paris I formed a musical group with Jacques Thibaud, who played the violin, and Alfred Cortot, who played the piano. The three of us played concerts and made recordings until 1937.

Now Susan and I lived more often in Europe, but she felt that she did not belong among my Catalan friends. She wanted to be in the United States and I wanted to stay in Spain, so we began to spend more time apart. Our marriage ended in 1928.

◆ ◆ ◆

In 1936, disaster came to Spain. General Franco led an army into Spain from Africa to take control of the government. A terrible <u>civil war</u> followed, and it lasted until 1939, when Franco became Spain's ruler. I had to shut down my Catalan orchestra and leave my home country. I moved to Prades in southern France, very near to the border with Spain.

Although war in Spain ended in the summer of 1939, another World War was just beginning in the rest of Europe. People in Europe now had to live with the sound of bombs, not music. I refused to play in any country that supported General Franco, or that was controlled by Hitler. I played only a few times during the war in <u>free</u> parts of France, and in Switzerland.

In 1950, five years after the end of the Second World War, I was persuaded to organize a music festival in Prades. It was 200 years since the death of J.S. Bach, and I was well known for playing Bach's cello works. I agreed, as long as the money from the tickets was sent to a hospital in the nearby town of Perpignan. Many excellent musicians came to Prades to play, and the festival was held every year after that. My music career had started again.

A young <u>violinist</u> from my mother's home country of Puerto Rico came to the festival in 1952. Her name was Marta Montáñez Martínez, and I was very <u>impressed</u> with her <u>talent</u>. I advised her to study in New York City, with teachers that I knew.

I was now busy with concerts and teaching in different cities, but my personal life was lonely. I had been friends for many years with Francesca Vidal de Capdevila, and I asked her to marry me. Sadly, she died a few months after our wedding, and I was alone again. I worked harder so that I did not have time to feel sad.

In 1956, when I was nearly 80 years old, I was invited to perform at the Casals Festival in Puerto Rico. Some of my mother's family still lived there, and I visited them. I also met Marta Montáñez again, who was now 19. We shared our love of music, and I became young again in her company. Many people did not approve of our relationship, but I asked her to marry me anyway. She agreed, and we were married for the next 16 years.

I lived in San Juan in Puerto Rico for the rest of my life, organizing the Puerto Rican Symphony Orchestra, and helping to set up the Puerto Rican Conservatory of Music. I was able to pass on the great history of Spanish music to new young musicians. The mix of Spanish and Puerto Rican music produced wonderful new styles, such as the *salsa*, *bomba* and *plena* sounds.

I continued to travel and give masterclasses in cities in the Americas and Europe. In 1961, I played again for the President of the United States, who at this time was John F. Kennedy. I was 85, and I was very pleased to play in the White House a second time, especially as the performance was recorded for radio and television.

I was invited to write a piece of music for the United Nations. It was first performed at the General Assembly in 1971, and I was the conductor. I was 95 years old! The UN awarded me their Peace Medal, and I spoke about my country. I told them I was Catalan, and that the world's first democratic parliament met in Catalonia. In my speech, I attacked Franco and his men, who had taken Spain's rights away.

Franco was still in control of Spain, and sadly he lived two years longer than me. Two years after my UN performance, in 1973, I died of old age at home in Puerto Rico. I did not live to see Spain become free again. I was very sad that war had driven me from the land of my birth. But I was very happy, and lucky, because I had loved and played music for more than 90 years.

The Life of Pablo Casals

1876   Pau (Pablo) Casals i Defilló was born in El Vendrell, Catalonia, Spain, on 29th December 1876. He was the second of eleven children.

1881   Aged five, Pablo joined a church choir. He had already learnt to play the piano, and soon he could also play the violin.

1888   He became a cello student at the Escola Municipal de Música in Barcelona, Spain. He was an excellent student.

1893   He moved to Madrid, where he entered the Real Conservatorio de Música y Declamación. He played in the Quartet Society, and gave concerts for the Queen Regent, Maria Cristina.

1895   He moved to Paris. He earned a living playing the cello in an orchestra in a musical theatre.

1896   Returning to Catalonia, he became a teacher at his old school, the Escola Municipal de Música in Barcelona. He also performed in the orchestra of the Gran Teatre del Liceu.

1897   Pablo performed with the Madrid Symphony Orchestra. He received a high honour – the Order of Carlos III – from Queen Maria Cristina.

1899   He visited England, where he played a public concert at London's Crystal Palace, and a private concert for Queen Victoria at her summer palace on the Isle of Wight. Later in the year, he made appeared at the Lamoureux Concerts in Paris. The audience loved him.

1900   A concert tour of Spain and Holland with the pianist Harold Bauer was a big success.

1901   Pablo crossed the Atlantic for the first time, and played concerts in the United States and South America.

1904   He played for the first time at Carnegie Hall in New York City, and then played for President Theodore Roosevelt at the White House in Washington DC.

1914   In the year that war broke out in Europe, Pablo married the American singer Susan Metcalfe.

1919   Pablo set up an orchestra in his home city of Barcelona, calling it *Orquesta Pau Casals*. It gave its first concert the following year.

1928   After 14 years Pablo and Susan decided to end their marriage.

1936   General Franco led the Army of Africa into
        Spain, taking control of Spain's government.
        The Spanish Civil War started, lasting until
        1939. Pablo hated Franco, and decided to
        shut down the Orquesta Pau Casals and leave
        Spain until democracy returned. He moved
        to France. Franco said he must never return
        to Spain. He never did.

1939–1942 Pablo moved to Prades, in southern France,
        near to the Spanish border. He performed
        at different places in southern France and
        Switzerland.

1945   After the war, he felt that Britain and the
        USA had abandoned Spain. They were too
        friendly to Franco. Pablo stopped performing.

1950   He started conducting and playing the cello
        again, performing at the Prades Festival. It was
        organized to celebrate two hundred years since
        the death of J. S. Bach. Pablo continued to
        lead the Prades Festivals until 1966.

1955   Pablo married his good friend, Francesca
        Vidal de Capdevila. Sadly, she died in the
        same year.

1956   Pablo moved to San Juan in Puerto Rico.

1957   Pablo married his pupil, Marta Montáñez
        Martínez.

1958   He started an orchestra – the Puerto Rico
        Symphony Orchestra – and, a year later, a
        music school, the Conservatory of Music of
        Puerto Rico.

1961   Pablo performed at the White House again,
        this time for President John F. Kennedy, who
        he admired.

1963   President Kennedy awarded Pablo the US
        Presidential Medal of Freedom.

1971   Approaching the great age of 95, Pablo
        performed his *Himno a las Naciones Unidas*
        (Hymn of the United Nations) at the
        General Assembly in New York City. He was
        awarded the United Nations Peace Medal.

1973   Pablo Casals died, aged 96, at home in San
        Juan, Puerto Rico.

Louis
Armstrong

◆ ◆ ◆

1901–1971

the American trumpet-player and singer

I was not born into a wonderful world. I grew up in a poor area of New Orleans, where life was <u>tough</u> for young African-American boys. But music saved me, and showed me that the world really was wonderful.

◆ ◆ ◆

I was born in 1901 in New Orleans, Louisiana, in the <u>Deep South</u> of the United States. Two years later, soon after my little sister was born, my father left the family. My mother didn't want to look after us on her own, so my sister and I went to live with Grandma Josephine. Although we had no toys, no shoes and very little food, my grandmother always sent us to school and to church.

When I was five, my mother returned and we lived with her. It wasn't a real home though, and I was often <u>on the streets</u>. I needed to earn money to buy food for my mother and sister, so I found a job delivering newspapers. But I started getting into trouble too. New Orleans was a tough city, and you had to join a street <u>gang</u> to survive. One of my jobs as a young member of the gang was to take messages, while another person was watching for enemy gangs outside clubs. I liked standing outside the clubs, because I could hear the music inside. <u>Ragtime</u> music was very popular then.

I found a job with a Jewish family from Russia. Their name was Karnofsky, and they used to buy and sell old furniture and other household things on the streets. Mr Karnofsky was very kind to me, and often invited me to stay in their house. Later, he also lent me enough money to buy a cornet, which is a kind of <u>trumpet</u>. He taught me how to live – to expect the best from people and myself, and to work hard.

I left school when I was 11 and joined a singing group of four boys. We earned a few dollars, singing the latest songs on street corners, and people seemed to like my voice. The other boys called me 'Satchel Mouth' because I had such a wide open mouth (a 'satchel' is a kind of school bag with a wide opening). Also, I learned to play some simple songs because some of the musicians in the clubs were kind to me and gave me music lessons.

Because of the area where I lived, I was often in trouble with the police. One New Year's Eve, when I was 11, I fired a gun into the air in the street. The police caught me, and sent me to the New Orleans Home for Colored <u>Waifs</u>, a home for young African-American boys who had been in trouble with the police. It was really a prison for children. I lived there for 18 months.

There was a music teacher at the Colored Waifs' Home called Professor Davis. Most of the other boys weren't interested in music and behaved badly in his lessons, but I wanted to learn. The Home had a band, and the band had a cornet, which I loved. I practised the cornet every day, improving all the time until, when I was only 13, Professor Davis asked me to be the leader of the band. It was the <u>proudest</u> day of my life.

When I left the Colored Waifs' Home I had nowhere to go and I was soon back on the streets again. I was 18, and I could have got into a lot of trouble. Life was kind to me, however. New Orleans was famous for its <u>brass band</u> parades. Brass bands walked through the streets of the town, playing popular songs. I soon found a job playing in these bands.

The city was also famous for its nightlife, with hundreds of clubs, <u>dance halls</u> and restaurants. When people heard me in the brass bands, they invited me to play in the clubs. I played with King Oliver, who was a fine cornet player and got me jobs with great jazz musicians. I joined a band on a Mississippi riverboat, playing as the boat went up and down the river. It was like a University of Music because the other musicians taught me to read music.

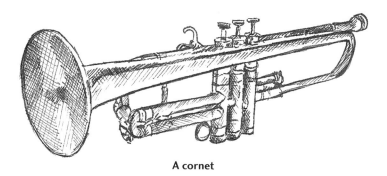

A cornet

I was ready to fall in love, and that's what happened when I met a girl called Daisy Parker. We married in 1918 and about that time, a cousin died. He had a three-year-old son who was called Clarence. Clarence had never recovered completely from a head injury and Daisy and I decided to give him a home, and he became Clarence Armstrong. Sadly, Daisy died at a very young age and I didn't feel I could look after Clarence alone. I put him into a special home, and paid for his care for the rest of his life.

◆ ◆ ◆

It was time for me to leave New Orleans and find out about the rest of the world. I was wondering where to go when King Oliver invited me to Chicago to join his Creole Jazz Band, and I moved to the big city. We played all night in the nightclubs. I played cornet and trumpet. Tough gangs controlled the clubs, and if you were a good musician, they paid you well. I was soon living in my own flat, driving a car and wearing fashionable clothes.

I started going out with Lil Hardin, who was the pianist in King Oliver's band. We married, and she decided to introduce me to other types of music. We went to concert halls to hear classical music and we went to church to learn how to play and sing gospel music. For the first time, I saw a different world which was not controlled by gangs.

Lil and I moved to New York City. I joined another band, and developed a new singing style, which I became famous for. I didn't sing words, but made sounds with my voice, using it like a musical instrument. In between songs, I told stories about life in New Orleans, which was very different from life on the East Coast. Our audience was mostly rich white people, and they loved me. I made lots of records and played with top jazz musicians.

The next year Lil and I returned to Chicago. We set up an orchestra, and I played the trumpet. It was a wonderful time. I played with famous <u>blues</u> and jazz musicians like Earl Hines, I made more recordings and I performed on popular radio shows. Lil and I were very busy, and we were beginning to live separate lives. I started a new group called Louis Armstrong and his Stompers. We played in a club called the Sunset Café, and the <u>gangster</u> Al Capone was often in the audience.

In 1929 I became involved in a musical show called *Hot Chocolate*, back in New York City. One of the songs from the show was 'Ain't Misbehavin'', which became a big hit for me. My name was becoming well known among jazz lovers. I played the trumpet and led the band in a nightclub in Harlem, the African–American area of New York City. The club was owned by a gangster called Dutch Schultz, and each night I played to big crowds. Favourite songs were 'Stardust' and 'Lazy River'. It was a great time to be in the city. But it did not last.

◆ ◆ ◆

In 1929, thousands of people lost all their money in the <u>Wall Street Crash</u>. Banks and businesses closed and millions of people lost their jobs. Nobody had money to spend and the clubs closed, too. It was time to move on, and I travelled right across the United States to Los Angeles, where the sun was always shining.

The Hollywood film industry was growing fast in Los Angeles. Many film people went to the New Cotton Club in the evenings, where the singer and film star Bing Crosby often sang. I began to perform there, too, and that led to the beginning of my career in films. I got into trouble with the police, however, and I had to leave Los Angeles. I went back to Chicago and New Orleans, but I was too close to the gangsters there and I didn't want more trouble with the police. Also, Lil and I decided to end our marriage at this time. What should I do and where could I go?

My <u>agent</u>, Johnny Collins, arranged a tour for me in Europe. I arrived in London in 1932, where a music journalist called Percy Brooks interviewed me about my life. I told him about singing on street corners in New Orleans when I was 11, and how the boys called me 'Satchel Mouth'. He loved the name, but changed it to the shorter name 'Satchmo', and it became my <u>nickname</u>.

Musically, the tour was a big success. Financially, it was a disaster. My agent was not a good agent, and when I got back to the United States, I needed to make some money fast. I went on a long tour, playing music to raise money. I was playing too much, however. My lips were sore and I needed a rest.

I decided to find a new agent and Joe Glaser, a Chicago gangster, took the job. He organized a band for me, and we played our first concert in Indianapolis in the summer of 1935. Over the next few years, I toured regularly with the band. I also found work acting in films and singing in the theatre, giving myself a rest from playing the trumpet. This was the age of radio, and I was the first African-American

to play on national radio in the United States. I was lucky in love, too, and, in 1942, I married Lucille Wilson, a dancer, who made me very happy. We moved to Queens, in New York City.

When the Second World War ended in 1945, it was the beginning of a new age. People wanted to enjoy themselves after the dark days of war. They crowded into cinemas, theatres and clubs. And if they stayed at home, they had a brand-new form of entertainment – television.

I wasn't a political person, but some things made me very angry. In 1957, in Little Rock, Arkansas, African-American and white children were not allowed to attend school together. I spoke about my anger, and refused to go on a tour to Russia because the United States State Department had organized it. The State Department is responsible for the relationship between the United States and countries abroad.

Time passed and I became an international star, appearing in films and playing concerts. I formed a new band called

Louis Armstrong and his All Stars, which performed all kinds of songs, not just jazz songs. In 1964, I recorded 'Hello, Dolly!', which I sang on a tour of Africa, Europe and Asia, and it became a hit in many countries.

I was working with the State Department again, and they often arranged and paid for my tours. This was the time of the Cold War between the two <u>superpowers</u> – the United States and the Soviet Union. The United States State Department tried to spread American culture around the world, and I worked for them. People called me 'Ambassador Satch'. I met people of all races and colours, and it made me think about my own life. Music had been my passport out of a very tough life. I had been very lucky.

In 1967, I recorded 'What a Wonderful World'. When I sang those words, I really meant them. My health was beginning to fail, however, and I had to spend some time in hospital. I died four years later, at my home in Corona, Queens, in New York City. I was 69.

The Life of Louis Armstrong

1901 Louis was born in New Orleans, Louisiana, the birthplace of jazz.

1903 Louis's father left the family. Louis and his younger sister lived with their grandmother, Josephine Armstrong.

1906 Louis and his sister returned to live with their mother. Louis started school.

1907 Aged just six years old, Louis worked for a Russian family, called the Karnofskys. They went round the streets selling second-hand furniture.

1912 Now 11, Louis left school. He joined a band with three other boys. They played on street corners.

1913 The police sent Louis to the Home for Colored Waifs for 18 months. The music teacher there taught Louis to play the cornet.

1914 Louis left the Home. He took a job delivering newspapers. Mr Karnofsky lent Louis money to buy his own cornet. Louis studied music with the cornet-player King Oliver, who played in the Kid Ory band. Louis found work playing in bands, in dance halls, on riverboats and in brass band parades in the city.

1918   When King Oliver moved to Chicago, Louis
        took his place as cornet player in the Kid Ory
        band. He met and fell in love with Daisy Parker.
        They married and took three-year-old Clarence,
        the son of Louis's cousin, into their home.

1919   Louis learnt how to read music. He joined
        the Tuxedo brass band as the second trumpet
        player.

1922   Daisy sadly died and Louis moved to Chicago
        to play second cornet in King Oliver's Creole
        jazz band. The next year, he made his first
        recordings and met Hoagy Carmichael.

1924   Louis married Lilian Hardin, the pianist in King
        Oliver's band. He moved to New York City to
        join an orchestra. He played on many recordings
        for blues singers, including Bessie Smith.

1925   Back in Chicago, Louis joined his wife's band,
        the Lil Hardin Armstrong band. He made
        his first recording with his own band, Louis
        Armstrong and his Hot Five.

1928–1930   Louis continued his career in New York City.
        'Ain't Misbehavin'' was a big hit. The United
        States banking crash happened in 1929, and
        many jazz clubs in New York City closed.
        Louis moved to Los Angeles. He played at the
        New Cotton Club there, and met film star,
        Bing Crosby.

1931   Louis and his wife Lil Hardin ended their marriage.

1931–1934   These were difficult years for Louis. In Chicago he had trouble with gangs. He toured Britain, Europe and the United States. He spent some time in Paris.

1935   In the United States, gangster Joe Glaser became Louis's manager. With Glaser's help, Louis became an international star.

1936   Louis appeared in the film *Pennies from Heaven* with Bing Crosby.

1937   He presented a television show, becoming the first African-American to host a national television programme in the United States.

1942   Louis married Lucille Wilson, a dancer at the Cotton Club.

1947–1956   Louis formed Louis Armstrong and his All Stars. He appeared in 30 Hollywood films and made many recordings. He appeared on the cover of *Time* magazine. He met the Pope in the Vatican in Rome. He appeared in the film *High Society*.

1957   Little Rock, Arkansas, refused to allow
        African-American and white children to
        attend school together. Louis spoke about
        his anger and refused to go on a tour to
        Russia because the US State department had
        organized it.

1964   His recording of Jerry Herman's song 'Hello,
        Dolly!' was a big success. He later appeared in
        the film *Hello, Dolly!* with Barbra Streisand.

1967   Louis recorded his most famous song, 'What a
        Wonderful World!' He wasn't well, and spent
        time in hospital.

1971   He died at his home in Corona, Queens, in
        New York City. He was 69.

Frank Sinatra

◆ ◆ ◆

1915–1998

the Italian-American singer and actor

I grew up in <u>tough</u> times on tough streets. I thank my parents for my amazing voice and bright blue eyes, which gave me a great career in <u>show business</u>.

♦ ◆ ♦

I was born on 12th December, 1915, in Hoboken, New Jersey. Hoboken is across the river from New York City. I was a very big baby and my birth was difficult. The doctor damaged my left ear, leaving me deaf in that ear.

I was the only child of Marty and Dolly. My father, who was a fireman, <u>boxer</u> and café owner, had come from Palermo in Sicily with his family in 1903. Dolly, my mother, was from northern Italy. Her job was nursing women who were having babies. She was a very noisy person, always talking and singing, and sometimes shouting. She had strong political views, too, especially about women's rights and she was very <u>ambitious</u> for me.

I was noisy, too, and I was always singing. I lived in a tough neighbourhood, so I joined in the street sports with the other boys. But I was really pretending to like sport, and I knew that I wanted to be a singer.

I went to high school for only 47 days so my education was short. The head teacher told me to leave because I behaved so badly. I had to get my education <u>on the streets</u>. This was the time of the Great Depression, following the Wall Street Crash of 1929 when many banks and businesses closed. Millions of people lost their jobs and many people also lost all their money. It was difficult to find enough food to survive. Local <u>gangs</u> took advantage of the situation, and there was a lot of crime.

Sometimes I was able to earn money with the gangs but I really wanted a proper job. I finally got one as a delivery boy for a newspaper called *The Jersey Observer*, which I enjoyed. I sang while I was delivering the newspapers, and some of my customers said that they liked my voice. There was a local group called The Three Flashes, and my mother persuaded them to let me join. We changed our name to The Hoboken Four and won first prize in a television <u>talent show</u>. The prize was a six-month <u>contract</u>, performing across the United States. Suddenly we were professional singers.

At home after the tour, I sang in the evenings at the Rustic Cabin, a club in New Jersey. By now, a few people in the music world knew my name. I loved listening to Bing Crosby, the singer and film star, on the radio. I took my girlfriend, Nancy, to see him when he gave a concert in New Jersey. I wanted to be on stage, singing, like Bing.

This was the age of big bands in <u>dance halls</u>, and Harry James invited me to sing with his band. I was earning $75 a week, and I was very <u>proud</u> of myself. I signed a contract with Harry, but when I received an offer from a bigger band, Harry let me leave. He was very kind to me, and a great help in my career. Things were going well for me, and I asked Nancy to marry me. She agreed, and we married in 1939.

◆ ◆ ◆

I joined the Tommy Dorsey <u>Orchestra</u>, and became his lead singer. The pay was much better, but I signed a bad contract with Tommy. My contract said that I had to give one-third of my earnings to Tommy, for the whole of my life. So when I left Tommy's band, my <u>agent</u> had to pay him a lot of money to end the contract.

There were more important battles than mine. The Second World War started in Europe in 1939. On 7th December 1941, the Japanese Air Force bombed Pearl Harbor in the US state of Hawaii, and the United States entered the war. Although I was not able to fight in the army because of my deafness, I performed shows for the soldiers who were going to Europe. In 1945, the fantastic news came through that the war was over. Our soldiers were coming home.

Nancy gave birth to our son, who was also called Frank, in 1944. My career continued to be successful, and I signed a contract with Columbia Records. My film career had started, too, and in 1945, I appeared in *Anchors Aweigh* with the Hollywood star, Gene Kelly. I also had the lead role in a short political film, called *The House I Live In*. It was about

<u>prejudice</u> against Jews and African-American people at the end of the Second World War. I won a special Academy Award (an 'Oscar®') for that film.

I <u>released</u> a new record in 1946, called *The Voice of Frank Sinatra*. It was popular with soldiers and their wives and girlfriends. I was loving life, singing, recording and acting full time. My third child, Tina, was born in 1948, but I was too busy to spend time with my family and my relationship with Nancy could not survive. In 1950, our marriage ended.

The next year, I married a famous actress, Ava Gardner. Photographers followed us everywhere, however, and we had no peace. Our pictures were always in the papers and our names were always on the radio. We were both very busy, but Ava was a bigger star than me. Perhaps I was too proud, and that affected our relationship.

I became <u>depressed</u>, too. Sometimes I felt very happy, and that everything was going well. Sometimes I felt as if I was in a black hole. My career had not been going well. There were stories in Hollywood that I was involved

Frank Sinatra's star on Hollywood Boulevard

with Italian <u>gangsters</u>, like Lucky Luciano. Although I did nothing against the law, it was true that some of my friends were gangsters. But they were my friends, and I liked them.

And then disaster came. I was doing a show at the Copacabana Club in New York City, when I tasted blood in my mouth. I had been singing too much, and I had damaged my voice. I was becoming less popular and I needed to sing to win more fans, but now I had to rest my voice. Was this the end of my career?

I was saved by new technology. Television arrived in the 1950s, bringing entertainment right into people's homes. People could now watch big shows, as well as listen to them on the radio. I was able to present *The Frank Sinatra Show*, and remind people who I was. When I sang on television, I could sing quietly without putting too much <u>strain</u> on my voice. It wasn't like singing in a large concert hall, and my voice became strong again. Although I was not a great success on television, the programme helped my career. Soon I was appearing in films again and I signed a recording contract with a company called Capitol Records.

The 1960s was a good decade for me. I produced lots of great singles and albums, working with amazing musicians, and I even started my own record company in 1961, called Reprise Records. A group of us – musicians and actors – became known as the Rat Pack, and I was called the 'Chairman of the Board', which meant that I was the leader. There were five of us in the Rat Pack, including singers Dean Martin and Sammy Davis Junior. We performed on stage in Las Vegas, singing, dancing and making jokes about each other, and we appeared together in films like *Ocean's Eleven*.

We got involved in politics, too. The Rat Pack supported the Democrats in American politics. The Democrats are the left-wing party and the Republicans are the right wing. Left-wing parties believe that government has an important role in creating a fair society; right-wing parties think that government should make as few laws as possible, and let people get on with their lives. We wanted John F. Kennedy to be President, and we worked hard for him in 1960. He won, and I organized the big concert on the evening before he moved into the White House. Lots of big show-business stars performed, and it was a great success.

I also sang at concerts to raise money for the <u>Civil Rights</u> movement, led by Martin Luther King. Dr King was fighting for <u>equal rights</u> for African-Americans and white Americans. At one show, while I was singing 'Old Man River', I saw tears in his eyes. I had worked all my life with African-American musicians, and I avoided hotels where they were not welcome.

◆ ◆ ◆

In the 1960s, I fell in love with the beautiful young actress Mia Farrow. Sadly, the marriage did not last, and we were only married for 18 months. We were always working in different places, and there was no time for us to be together.

I had a big <u>scare</u> in my life in 1963, when my son, Frank Junior, aged 19, was <u>kidnapped</u> by some criminals. I paid a large amount of money to them, and after four days, they <u>released</u> him. He was fine, but it was a tough experience for the family. The police caught the kidnappers, and sent them to prison.

My daughter Nancy had started on her singing career, and we often sang together. We recorded 'Something Stupid', which was a big hit. I also performed many times with the great jazz singer, Ella Fitzgerald. In 1969, a friend called Paul Anka sent me a new song. I wasn't feeling very happy and it made me feel better. It was called 'My Way', and it became my most famous song. The words were perfect for me. It was about a man who's had a great life. Good things and bad things have happened but he <u>regrets</u> nothing.

Then the old stories about my gangster friends appeared in the newspapers again. I felt angry when I read them and I repeated that I could choose my own friends. There is always trouble where there are gangsters, and I was silly. I got into a big argument in Caesar's Palace, a hotel in Las Vegas, and the manager there tried to shoot me. Luckily, he missed, but it made me think about what was important in life. After 36 years in show business, I decided to retire.

I soon became bored, however, and decided to record a new album. I called it *Ol' Blue Eyes is Back*, because my favourite <u>nickname</u> was 'Ol' Blue Eyes' (Ol' means Old). The album did well and I decided to go on tour. The newspapers were not kind to me in Australia, however, and I got into trouble after arguing with the journalists. I called them some terrible names, and I had to apologize. Luckily, Europe was more welcoming, but I performed many concerts in a short space of time and I was very tired at the end of it.

In 1976, at home in Palm Springs in Los Angeles, I asked my neighbour and friend Barbara Marx to marry me. We enjoyed each other's company, and we shared the same interests. Over the next decade, we toured the world and raised millions of dollars for charity. It was a happy time. I had started making films again, too, but I didn't have very much energy now. I made my last film, called *First Deadly Sin*, in 1980. Many people think of me as a singer, but I made more than 30 films in my career.

As I had got older, my political opinions had changed and I now supported the right-wing Republican candidate for the US Presidency, Ronald Reagan. I gave $4 million to Reagan's campaign, and organized a big concert for him.

In 1980, I made a new recording of one of my most famous songs, 'New York, New York'. I gave my final concert in Japan in 1994, although I still sang at private parties. I had always loved playing golf, and I spent many of my last days on a golf course with friends. In 1998, I died at home in Palm Springs. I was 82.

Some people had loved me. Some people had hated me. But I had certainly lived my life in my own way.

The Life of Frank Sinatra

1915   Frank was born in Hoboken, New Jersey, across the Hudson River from Manhattan in New York. He was the only child of Italian parents.

1929   Frank went to Demarest High School, Hoboken, for 47 days. He became a newspaper delivery boy. He met his future wife, Nancy Barbato.

1933   Frank got a job as a sports reporter.

1935   His mother, Dolly, persuaded a local group called The Three Flashes to let Frank join them. They became the Hoboken Four. They went on a TV talent show, and won first prize. They signed a six-month contract to perform around the USA.

1939   He made his first recording, signing a one-year contract. Harry James, who had a band, heard Frank on the radio and asked him to join his band. Frank married Nancy Barbato.

1940   Tommy Dorsey invited Frank to join his orchestra. Frank made his first film appearances, in *Las Vegas Nights* and *Ship Ahoy*. Frank was singing in Hollywood when Nancy gave birth to their first child, also called Nancy. Like her father, Nancy had a successful singing and acting career.

1942–1944 He began his career as a <u>solo</u> artist, signing a contract with Columbia Records.

1944 His son, also called Frank, was born, and the family moved to Los Angeles.

1945 Frank appeared with Gene Kelly in the film *Anchors Aweigh*. He also acted in a ten-minute film called *The House I Live in*. He received a special Oscar for it.

1946 He released his first album, *The Voice of Frank Sinatra*, and began his own weekly radio show.

1948 His career was not very successful. Newspaper articles said that Frank was involved with Italian gangsters, like Lucky Luciano. His third child with Nancy was born. They called her Tina.

1950 Frank damaged his voice and had to rest it. Television saved his career, and he presented his own television show for two years. His marriage to Nancy ended.

1951 He married the actress Ava Gardner.

1953 He signed a recording contract with Capitol Records. Frank and Ava's marriage ended after 18 months.

1954–1958   He won an Oscar for Best Supporting Actor, for his role in the film *From Here to Eternity*. His album *Come Fly with Me* was a hit.

1960   Frank and a few friends, including Dean Martin and Sammy Davis Junior, became known as 'The Rat Pack'. They appeared together on stage in Las Vegas. They starred together in the film, *Ocean's Eleven*.

1963   Frank Junior, now aged 19, was kidnapped. Frank paid a large amount of money to the kidnappers, and Frank Jr was released four days later. The kidnappers went to prison.

1966   Frank married actress Mia Farrow. The marriage ended after two years.

1967   Frank and daughter Nancy produced a hit record together. It was called 'Something Stupid'.

1969   He recorded his most famous song, 'My Way'. It was a hit all over the world.

1971   He retired.

1973   After two years of retirement, Frank was bored. He re-started his career with an album called *Ol' Blue Eyes is Back*.

1976   Frank married Barbara Marx, his
       neighbour in Palm Springs. Their marriage
       lasted until his death.

1980   He made a new recording of one of his
       most famous songs, 'New York, New
       York'. He changed his political opinions,
       supporting the Republican candidate for
       the US Presidency, Ronald Reagan. He
       gave $4 million to Reagan's campaign,
       and organized a big concert for President
       Reagan.

1985   He received the Medal of Freedom from
       President Ronald Reagan.

1994   He gave his final public concert.

1998   Frank died, aged 82, at his home in Los
       Angeles.

Edith Piaf

◆ ◆ ◆

1915–1963

France's famous singing star

When I was born my parents did not want me. Nobody loved me when I was a child. I earned my food by singing in the street. And then, one evening on a Paris street, a nightclub owner heard my voice and tears filled his eyes.

♦ ◆ ♦

My name was Édith Giovanna Gassion and my life did not begin well. I was born in France in the middle of the First World War, on 15th December 1915. My parents didn't want me. They were young and enjoying life, and a child was not part of their plans. Annetta, my mother, was Italian, with North African parents. She sang in cafés. Louis, my father, was a street performer.

My mother left me with her mother in Paris. In 1916, my father joined the army, but before he went to fight, he came to see me. He was unhappy when he saw me because I was sick, and he felt that my grandmother wasn't looking after me properly. He decided to take me to live with his mother in Normandy. Although she was kinder to me, my health didn't improve. In fact, I developed an eye infection, and I began to lose my eyesight, which was very frightening. I couldn't see for four years.

When I was 14, I became my father's assistant in his street performance. <u>Papa</u> was an <u>acrobat</u> and there was a monkey in his show. I had two jobs. I had to collect money in a hat from the audience after each show, and I had to look after the monkey. If Papa liked a town, we sometimes stayed there for a while, and I could go to the local school. But we never stayed more than a few weeks, and soon we were travelling again. We were very poor, and I often had no shoes.

One cold winter's day, Papa was ill. We had no money and nothing to eat, so I went to the town centre. It was market day and I put our collecting hat on the ground. I only knew one song – the French national song, which is called 'La Marseillaise'. I sang with great feeling, as if I was trying to save Papa's life. People stopped to listen and I saw tears in their eyes. The hat filled with money, far more than we ever got for Papa's show.

Papa was very pleased, and after that, I always sang at the beginning of his show. I sang in the open air, like a bird. I couldn't read very well, and it was hard to learn the words. But I loved entertaining the crowds, who usually wanted to hear more songs when I'd finished singing.

By the time I was 15, I knew I wanted to be a singer. It was time to leave Papa's show, and start working on my own. He had done his best for me, and although I was sad to leave him, I was excited too.

I set off for Paris. In 1929, thousands of people lost all their money in the <u>Wall Street Crash</u> in the United States. Banks and businesses closed and millions of people lost their jobs. This had a big effect in Europe, and the 1930s were difficult years for everyone. I found a cheap hotel in an area of Paris called Montmartre, and then walked down a hill to an area called Pigalle.

There, I made friends with a homeless girl called Mômone, and I explained that I planned to earn money by singing. She offered to collect money in a hat while I sang. The plan worked, although we didn't earn much money. We toured the city, staying in different hotels, but sometimes we had to sleep in the <u>doorways</u> of shops.

One night, we went to a café with the money we had collected. I met a boy called Louis Dupont, who was very funny. He was 17 and worked as a delivery boy. I fell in love with him as he showed me beautiful parts of the city. Unhappily, I discovered that I was expecting a baby and, just like my own mother, I didn't know how to look after a child.

Soon after our daughter Marcelle was born, I started singing again. I was often out all night, working and enjoying myself afterwards in the clubs. Louis stayed at home and looked after the baby. But then she fell ill, with a terrible disease called meningitis. There was no medicine for it in those days, and she died. She was two years old. Louis and I didn't want to be together after that, and our relationship ended.

I was very sad about Louis and the baby, and I looked for a new set of friends. I met a man called Albert, who spent his time with criminals, and wasn't as kind as Louis. I soon learned that Albert didn't really love me – he wanted me to make money for him by singing. He collected crowds to hear me sing in the street, and took half of the money which I earned. He used to hit me too, so I left him. He said he was going to shoot me because I had left him, but I was strong, and I didn't go back to him.

One evening, while I was singing in Pigalle I noticed a well-dressed man in the crowd. His name was Louis Leplée and he owned a nightclub called Le Gerny. He asked me to come and <u>audition</u> for him. That performance was my first experience of singing on a real stage, and I was nervous. But Louis liked me and my voice, and he gave me a job.

There was a lot of work to do before my first performance, however. I was tiny – only 1.42 metres tall and very thin – and my clothes and hair looked terrible. Louis bought me a simple black dress and took me to the hairdresser's. He showed me how to stand and move on the stage, and he even gave me my name. He called me 'la môme piaf', which means 'the little sparrow'. The sparrow is the most common bird in the world, and loves to live near humans. First it was my <u>nickname</u>, and later it <u>became</u> my stage name – Edith Piaf. It was easy to say and hard to forget.

My first performance was a great success, and I soon signed a <u>contract</u> to make two records. Louis was happy for me. At Le Gerny I earned more money than I had ever seen, and I used my money to entertain my friends at the clubs and restaurants in Pigalle.

◆ ◆ ◆

And then, one terrible day in 1936, some <u>gangsters</u> shot Louis dead. They were people I had known in the past, and the police believed that I was part of their <u>gang</u>. The story was in the newspapers, and people didn't support me. I needed help and I got help from Raymond Asso, a songwriter and nightclub owner. He was born in Morocco and had been in the <u>French Foreign Legion</u>, which was a very <u>tough</u> section of the French army. He had already written songs for me, but now we fell in love.

It seemed a good idea to leave Paris for a while, so I went on tour around France. It worked – I became famous. When I returned to Paris in the late 1930s, I saw my name in lights – in big letters on the front of the concert hall where I was singing. The Second World War started in 1939, and Raymond joined the army, ending our relationship. I began a career in the theatre, starring in a play by Jean Cocteau, called *Le Bel Indifférent*, in 1940.

Then the Nazis drove into Paris and the German army took control of our beautiful city and most of France. Our wonderful life in Paris was over for now. I found a new manager called Andrée Bigard, who helped me a lot, organizing shows for French prisoners in the German prisons. Some of them were able to dress as members of the <u>orchestra</u>, and escape.

I continued to sing during the war. Sometimes, I sang for Nazi officers, and people said I was a collaborator – a person who helps the enemy. But actually I was helping the <u>Resistance</u> – the French men and women fighting secretly against the Nazis.

During these dangerous times, I became friends with Marguerite Monnot, a songwriter. As the war was ending, Marguerite and I wrote a song together. It was called 'La

Edith's name in lights

Vie en Rose' and it became a hit around the world. I sang it in America, when I went on tour there with a singer called Charles Aznavour, after the war. My shows in New York City sold out.

♦ ◆ ♦

I had looked for love all my life. I found it again after I returned to Europe from the United States. I met a man called Marcel Cerdan, who was a <u>boxer</u>. We fell in love and set our wedding date. Before we could marry, however, I had more concerts to sing in America and I flew back to New York City.

I performed my concerts well, but all the time I was thinking about Marcel. A few days later, he boarded a plane in Paris to fly to me in New York City. He never arrived. His plane crashed into the ocean, killing him and everyone on board. His death made me very unhappy.

Just two years later, I was in an accident, too. I broke both my arms in a car crash, and spent a lot of time in hospital. This was a difficult time for me – I had many health problems, including <u>addictions</u>, and I really missed Marcel. I kept looking for love and in 1952, I married a singer called Jacques Pills. He was a good friend and he tried to help me with my addictions, but I was not easy to live with, and our marriage ended after a few years.

I felt that I was going mad. I thought about Marcel all the time. The only good thing in my life was singing. I still loved to perform and entertain my fans. My favourite place to perform was the Paris Olympia music hall where I sang every year from 1955 to 1962. I was also looking for the perfect song. I was sent hundreds of songs, and most of them were terrible.

Then one day in 1960, two songwriters visited me. Their names were Charles Dumont and Michel Vaucaire, and they gave me the words for a song. As soon as I read the title, I knew it was my song: 'Non, je ne regrette rien', which means 'No, I don't <u>regret</u> anything'. I first performed it at the Paris Olympia in January 1961. As I sang the final note, everyone in the audience jumped to their feet, clapping and asking me to sing it again. It became my most famous song.

In 1962, I married a Greek singer, Theo Sarapo, who was twenty years younger than me. My health wasn't very good, I was always in pain, and nothing seemed to help. Then the doctor told me the terrible news that I had cancer. I died in 1963, at my home on the <u>French Riviera</u>. So my life was short but I had lived an exciting life. I started life as a little girl that nobody wanted – at the end of my life, people loved me around the world. I regretted nothing.

The Life of Edith Piaf

1915   Edith was born as Édith Giovanna Gassion, in Paris. Her parents did not want to look after her and she lived with her grandmother.

1918   Edith had an eye infection and could not see for four years.

1929   When she was 14, Edith joined her father's street show. They travelled all over France. Edith sang for the first time in public.

1931   Edith met a delivery boy called Louis Dupont, and they fell in love. A year later, Edith gave birth to a daughter, Marcelle. Aged two, she suddenly developed meningitis and died.

1935   A nightclub owner heard Edith sing and persuaded her to sing in his club. His name was Louis Leplée, and he gave Edith the nickname 'La môme piaf', which means 'the little sparrow'. Edith changed her stage name to Edith Piaf. She made two records.

1936   Louis Leplée was shot dead. Edith met Raymond Asso, who owned a nightclub and wrote songs. He started to write for Edith, and they fell in love.

1940   She appeared in a play by Jean Cocteau.
        She became one of France's most popular
        performers during the war.

1944   She discovered a young male singer called
        Yves Montand. She invited him to sing
        with her on stage.

1945   Edith recorded her famous song, 'La vie
        en rose'. At the end of the war, Edith
        began to tour the world. She was soon an
        international star.

1948   She met the boxer, Marcel Cerdan.

1949   Marcel was killed in a plane crash, while
        flying from Paris to New York City to
        meet Edith.

1951   Edith herself was involved in an accident.
        She was in a car with singer Charles
        Aznavour when they crashed. She broke
        both her arms.

1952   She married Jacques Pills.

1956   Edith's marriage to Jacques ended after four
        years. She performed at Carnegie Hall in
        New York City.

1960   Two songwriters came to see her with a
        new song. It was called 'Non, je ne regrette
        rien'. She first performed it at the Paris
        Olympia music hall the following year. It
        became her most famous song.

1962   She married a young singer, Theo Sarapo.
        They went on tour together, but Edith was
        not well.

1963   Edith recorded her last song, 'L'homme de
        Berlin'. She died in her villa on the French
        Riviera.

Maria Callas

◆ ◆ ◆

1923–1977

the Greek opera singer

**I had no time to play or make friends as a child.
I practised music day and night. When I was 16, war
came to Europe. Finally, when I was 21, I was able to
start my brilliant career.**

◆ ◆ ◆

I was born on 2nd December 1923 at a hospital in a
very expensive area of New York City – Fifth Avenue,
Manhattan – but my parents were not rich. They were not
Americans either. They had arrived from Greece in 1923,
looking for a better life, like so many other families. I was
born four months later.

My mother, Evangelia, was not pleased to see me. I was
her third child, and she wanted a son. She had had a son,
but he had died the year before from meningitis, a terrible
illness in those days. Now she was left with my older sister,
Yakinthi, and me. She refused to look at me for four days,
but she learnt to love me and later became <u>devoted</u> to me.

The family first noticed that I loved music when I was about three. By the time I was five, I often had to sing for friends and family, and I hated it. Piano lessons were arranged when I was nine, music teachers were found for me, and I was taken from one music class to another. I practised before and after school and my mother entered me for every music competition she could find. When I was 11, I won a singing competition on the radio. There was no time for me to be a child.

My mother was devoted to her daughters, but she was not devoted to my father, George. They were very different from each other, and the marriage was not a good one. George took life easy and liked to enjoy himself, and he never worried about the future. Although Evangelia was very <u>ambitious</u>, she had not wanted to go to America. She was not happy there and because George was not sympathetic to her feelings, she prepared to leave.

So when I was 14, my sister and I suddenly found ourselves in Greece, which was a strange country to us. We had to speak a different language and learn a new way of life. My mother continued to control my life, and I worked hard to please her. I <u>auditioned</u> for the Athens Conservatoire, which was the best music school in Greece. Because I was not a trained singer, however, the teachers weren't <u>impressed</u> by my voice. And they didn't like me also because I was too fat and wore glasses.

So my mother took me to a different college. She took me to the Greek National Conservatoire, where I auditioned again. This time, one of the teachers, Maria Trivella, thought there was something special about my voice. She said it was amazing. She offered to teach me and did not ask my mother to pay for the lessons.

I trained for six or seven hours each day for six months, until I was able to sing an 'aria'. An aria is an opera song for one voice. This aria was from Puccini's opera, *Tosca*. I continued studying with Maria for two years, and then my mother arranged a second audition at the Athens Conservatoire. This time, they gave me a place. I began to study with the great Spanish <u>soprano</u>, Elvira de Hidalgo.

I was 16 years old and ready to take control of my own life. I was a teenager, and I wanted my freedom. But suddenly Europe started to lose its freedom, when the Second World War started in September 1939. Normal life did not stop at first, and I was able to sing at the Royal Theatre in Athens. But in April 1941, when German and Italian soldiers invaded Greece, our lives became terrible. We could not get food, and the only people with any money were the soldiers.

If Greek girls went out with German soldiers, they had to be very careful because the Greek <u>Resistance</u> was watching. I concentrated on my singing. Music performances were allowed, but most people were worrying about food, not opera. In 1942, I sang for the first time as a professional singer. The opera was Suppé's *Boccaccio*, and we performed it at the Lyric Theatre in Athens. I sang in other productions, including *Tosca*, *Cavalleria Rusticana* by Mascagni and Beethoven's *Fidelio*. The newspapers liked my performances.

When the Germans and Italians left Greece in 1944, I was 21. I was invited to sing at the Parthenon, the classical Greek <u>temple</u> built more than 2,300 years before on a hill above Athens, which was a very emotional moment for me.

◆ ◆ ◆

After the war ended, Elvira thought I should sing in Italy. I was not sure because Italy had been our enemy during the war and the cities were in <u>ruins</u>. I decided instead to return to the United States, where the cities and the people were alive and well. The war had not damaged America, and everyone there was ready to spend money and have a good time.

I did not manage my career well, however. I had an audition at New York's Metropolitan Opera (the 'Met'), which went well. The Met offered me a <u>contract</u>, but I didn't like the list of <u>roles</u> that they offered me. I decided to say no, thinking that I had a better offer from an opera house in Chicago, to sing in another Puccini opera – *Turandot*. But there were financial problems with *Turandot*, and the performances didn't happen. Now what was I going to do?

<u>Maestro</u> Serafin, a famous opera <u>conductor</u>, was looking for a soprano to sing in the big outdoor theatre in Verona in Italy. He auditioned me in Chicago, and found that I was <u>confident</u> and had a big voice. I got the role. I sailed back across the Atlantic to Italy. In Verona, I met a rich Italian businessman, called Giovanni Battista Meneghini. He loved opera and we soon fell in love. After we married in 1949, Giovanni became my manager.

One of my early roles was at the Teatro la Fenice in Venice, where I performed in *Die Walküre* by Wagner, again for Maestro Serafin. It was hard work, and I wanted a rest after our final performance. Six days later, another opera production was going to start. Maestro Serafin was very upset because his soprano for this production had become ill and he came to see me. It was a Bellini opera called *I Puritani*, which was completely different from Wagner. I didn't know the role and I didn't know if I could learn it in six days. But I agreed to sing the role.

Everyone in Italy knows about opera, and the newspapers said Maestro Serafin was taking a big <u>risk</u>. An unknown Greek soprano could not sing the role of Elvira, they wrote. I worked day and night. My heart was beating very fast as I stepped onto the stage. But I was confident, because I knew I was a good singer. I was a great success. The audience loved me, and after that role I became a famous soprano.

My husband helped my brilliant career. In 1951, I sang at La Scala in Milan, the world's most famous opera house, where I worked with many wonderful musicians. One was the singer Franco Corelli, who I met in 1953 – we formed a wonderful singing partnership. I also worked with the famous directors Visconti and Zeffirelli. And I signed a recording contract and developed my recording career.

La Scala opera house, Milan, Italy

I knew I had problems with my weight but I was shocked when Maestro Serafin told me I was eating too much. When I weighed myself, I realized that he was right. I began to eat more carefully, and I became much thinner. I could sing new roles and I felt more confident about my appearance. And in 1956, I finally made my debut in the United States of America, singing the part of Norma in Bellini's *Norma* at New York's Metropolitan Opera. Unfortunately, I argued with the General Manager, Rudolf Bing, and the Met ended my contract after two years.

Plenty of other opera houses invited me to sing, including London's Royal Opera House, but people were beginning to say that I was difficult. The newspapers called me a 'diva'. Everything had to be exactly as I wanted it, they said. If I didn't like something, I became angry, like a small child. In Rome in 1958, for example, I couldn't finish a performance for the President of Italy because I was unwell. The newspapers were very unfair to me, and said that I had left angrily. But I was an artist! I had to perform at my best, or not at all.

My marriage to Giovanni ended after ten years, and I was sad about this. And then I met Aristotle Onassis, a Greek businessman who owned a shipping company. He was very kind to me and because of him, I began to love life again. I loved sailing on his beautiful yacht. We ate at the best restaurants and went to the most fashionable places. When I stepped off the yacht on the French Riviera, I felt like the queen of the world.

During this time, I gave fewer performances but I accepted the big roles. I sang in *Tosca* for Franco Zeffirelli at the Royal Opera House in London and in Bellini's *Norma* at the Paris Opera. The following year I returned to the Met in New York. But my voice was beginning to feel tired. My last major appearance was at a performance for the Queen of England in 1965 in London.

I was expecting to retire and marry Aristotle. I was just 45. Then I had a terrible <u>shock</u>. Aristotle had fallen in love with Jackie Kennedy, the widow of John F. Kennedy, President of the USA. They married, and she became Mrs Onassis, not me.

I had to make changes in my life, so I took a singing role in a film and I taught <u>masterclasses</u> in New York. I met an old friend, Giuseppe di Stefano, and we decided to go on tour together, singing arias from favourite operas. We raised a lot of money for a medical charity, touring in the United States, Europe and Japan. I was living a good life again.

For many years I had been careful about my food. I had lost a lot of weight. It was good for my health and my appearance, but less good for my voice. Now in my fifties, I could not sing like a 20-year-old any more.

My career was over. I moved into an apartment in Paris, and lived quietly, away from the <u>glamorous</u> world of opera and performances. I began to feel unwell, and the doctors found that my heart was not strong. I died in Paris in 1977. Although I died alone, I was happy that I had been able to sing for so many people around the world.

The Life of Maria Callas

1923   Maria was born in 1923 in New York City. Her parents, George and Evangelia, came from Greece.

1927   Her father opened a pharmacy, moving the family from Queens to Manhattan.

1929   The family surname was Kalogeropoulos. Americans found it difficult to say or spell, so Maria's father changed it to Callas.

1932   Maria began piano lessons. Her mother immediately realized that Maria was good at music. Two years later, Maria won a radio singing competition.

1937   Maria's parents decided to end their marriage, and Evangelia took her daughters, Maria and Yakinthi, back to Athens, the capital of Greece. Maria trained to be a soprano singer at the Greek National Conservatoire, and performed for the first time in public the next year, singing an aria from the opera *Tosca*.

1939   The Second World War started. While she was still a student, Maria performed in her first full opera, *Cavalleria Rusticana* by Mascagni, at the Olympia Theatre in Athens. She studied with Elvira de Hidalgo, a well-known Spanish soprano.

1942   Maria appeared for the first time as a professional singer in *Boccaccio*. She played leading roles in *Tosca* and *Tiefland* by Eugen d'Albert.

1945   At the end of the war, Maria gave a final concert in Athens before returning to the United States.

1947   Maria sang at the Verona Opera Festival, her first performance in Italy. The following year, in Florence, she sang in *Norma*. The aria 'Casta Diva' from the opera became her most famous aria.

1949   She married Giovanni Meneghini, who was a rich Italian businessman. She performed in Buenos Aires in Argentina, and in Venice in Italy.

1951   Maria performed at the famous opera house, La Scala, in Milan in Verdi's opera *I Vespri Siciliani*. The next year she went to London, and signed a recording contract with EMI.

1953   Maria met the Italian singer, Franco Corelli. They became singing partners.

1954   She lost a lot of weight and changed her appearance completely. She performed in *Norma* in Chicago in the United States.

1956   Maria appeared on the cover of *Time* magazine. She finally performed at New York's Metropolitan Opera, singing the part of Norma again.

1958   She gave her first performance at the Paris Opera. The President of France, René Coty, was in the audience.

1959   Maria and her husband Giovanni ended their marriage of ten years. Maria met Aristotle Onassis, a Greek businessman who owned a shipping company.

1964   After a break from performing, Maria returned to the stage in London, Paris and New York.

1965   Maria gave her final opera performance in *Tosca* at Covent Garden in London, before retiring from concert singing.

1968   Aristotle Onassis married Jackie Kennedy, the widow of President John F. Kennedy. Maria was shocked and upset when she heard the news.

1969   She appeared in her first film, a production of *Medea*.

1971   She gave masterclasses at a music school in New York City. She met an old colleague, Giuseppe de Stefano. They became close friends.

1973   Maria and Giuseppe went on tour in America, Europe and Japan, performing concerts to raise money for a medical charity.

1974   She gave her final concert in Sapporo, Japan. Her partnership with Giuseppe ended.

1977   Maria was living alone in Paris when she died, aged 53.

Elvis Presley

◆ ◆ ◆

1935–1977

the man who changed pop music

**My twin brother died, my father went to prison,
we lost our home and I had a <u>stammer</u>. But then
I started to sing <u>gospel</u> music in church, and I was
given a guitar for my birthday. When I sang and
played, all my troubles disappeared.**

◆ ◆ ◆

I was born on 8th January 1935, and the day was happy and
sad. My mother, Gladys, gave birth to me, a healthy baby
son. But her second son, my identical twin, died during the
birth. I grew up without brothers or sisters.

I was born in Tupelo in Mississippi, in the <u>Deep South</u>
of the United States. We lived in a <u>shack</u> with two rooms.
It was very small, but it was our home. Then one day, when
I was three years old, my mother said we had to pack our
things and leave. My father, Vernon, was in trouble. He'd
tried to steal eight dollars, and the <u>judge</u> sent him to prison

for eight months. My mother had no money, and we had to stay with relatives.

Perhaps this difficult start in life was the reason for my stammer. When I tried to speak, I couldn't say the words. Other kids laughed at me at school. My mother told me not to listen to them. I found help with my stammer in church, where we sang gospel songs. 'Gospel' is the kind of music that you hear in African-American churches. When I joined in the singing, I didn't stammer at all. I could sing the words easily.

I only did well in one lesson at school – music! The music teacher said I had a good voice, and she entered me for a singing competition. I was 10 years old, I came fifth and I won five dollars! That competition was important in my life, not because I won five dollars, but because I felt confident in public. I felt confident for the first time in my life.

For my eleventh birthday, I asked my parents for a bicycle but instead, they bought me a guitar. My uncle taught me to play, and I practised every day. I listened to pop songs on the local Tupelo radio station, and learned how to play them.

In 1948, we moved to Memphis, Tennessee, where my father hoped to find work. Memphis was the home of the music styles that I loved – gospel, soul, blues and a new sound, rock and roll. I never went anywhere without my guitar. Sometimes, in cafés, people asked me to sing and they seemed to like my voice.

I had trouble at my new school, however. Some of the kids were unkind and laughed at the music I played. I didn't listen to them. Each year at the school there was a talent competition. After my performance in 1953, all the students stood up and clapped, especially the girls. I won!

When I finished high school that same year, I became a truck driver, a job that I loved. I was outdoors all day, listening to the radio, singing the songs and getting a good musical education. On Memphis radio they played the blues, African-American music and songs from singers like Frank Sinatra. I heard the latest jazz sounds in nightclubs in town, and I still sang gospel in church.

Soon after I started my job, I went to a place called Sun Records, a studio in town, where you could make a record for two dollars. I made two records, which I gave to my mother as a present. Then Sam Philips, who owned Sun Records, introduced me to two other musicians, Scotty Moore and Bill Black. We recorded some songs together. During a break, I played a song called 'That's All Right Mama', just for fun. But Sam said it was exactly what he wanted – a new type of pop music. We recorded it.

When 'That's All Right Mama' was played on the radio, lots of people wanted to talk to Sam. They all wanted to know who the singer was. We formed a band called the Blue Moon Boys, and we played our first concert on a hot summer evening. I was very nervous and I couldn't keep my legs still, so I shook my legs in time to the music. The girls in the audience went <u>crazy</u>. We began to get <u>bookings</u>, and I decided to leave my job.

I became more confident, and danced on stage, moving my <u>hips</u> from side to side. The girls loved it, but their parents were not <u>impressed</u>. When local newspapers wrote angry stories about me, Sam was pleased. He said it was good for my career, because people were talking about me. Sun Studios <u>released</u> ten songs, and more <u>dance halls</u> booked us.

◆ ◆ ◆

In 1956, I met <u>Colonel</u> Tom Parker, who wanted to be my manager. He'd already managed some successful music stars in Memphis, and we signed a <u>contract</u>. With Colonel Parker as my manager, I became successful too. He arranged a record contract with RCA Victor Records.

I went to Nashville, Tennessee, a city which is famous for <u>country music</u>. I recorded a song called 'Heartbreak Hotel', which was a big success. I sang with a group called the Jordanaires. With their gospel-style voices, we made a great <u>sound</u>. We recorded my first album, called *Elvis Presley*. Suddenly I was famous. That same year, I began my film career, starring in *Love Me Tender*.

Not everyone liked my sound, however. Some radio <u>DJs</u> thought I was an African-American singer, and they refused to play my music. There was a huge amount of <u>prejudice</u> against African-Americans in the Deep South in the 1950s. They still had to give their seats to white people on public buses in some states, like Alabama. A year before, in 1955, an African-American woman called Rosa Parks had refused to give her seat to a white man. That was in Montgomery, Alabama and it was an important moment in the fight to win <u>equal rights</u> for African-Americans.

I appeared on television and sang a song called 'Hound Dog'. My dancing <u>shocked</u> the nation. News reporters asked me to explain what I was doing. Rock and roll was

JAILHOUSE ROCK

a new kind of music, I told them, and you had to dance to it in a new way. One judge in Jacksonville said I was a danger to young people. But it was too late. Young fans loved my dancing, and started to copy it in dance halls all over America. People wanted me to appear on national television shows, but they didn't want to upset their older viewers. They decided I could appear on television, but the cameras only showed the top half of my body.

I received lots of love letters every day. When I was in town, thousands of girls waited for hours to see me. Guards were employed to control them. My record company had never seen sales like mine.

The success of *Love Me Tender* had started my film career at the same time. Instead of playing more concerts, I made films. 'You can appear in every town on the same night if you make films,' said Colonel Parker. So I appeared in *Jailhouse Rock*, *Loving You* and *King Creole* over the next 18 months.

Fans and photographers followed me everywhere. I decided to buy a mansion – a very big house – called Graceland, in Memphis. It had lots of land, and became a place where I could have some peace. My parents needed a more private place, too, and they moved in. What a difference from our little shack in Tupelo!

Then, suddenly, my career stopped because I had to join the army. We were in the middle of the <u>Cold War</u> between the world's two <u>superpowers</u> – the United States of America and the Soviet Union. There was no actual fighting, but both sides kept soldiers ready to fight. I was sent to Germany where my life was very different. Now I wasn't Elvis, the rock and roll star – I was Presley, Army Private 53310761!

My mother became very ill while I was in Germany and I was allowed home for a visit. Sadly, she died. She was only 46, and I was very upset. I had problems with <u>depression</u> later in life, and they started at this time.

I returned to army life in Germany. We didn't get much <u>free</u> time, but one evening I organized a party at my home. One of my guests was Priscilla Beaulieu, a girl from a military family. Although she was only 14, I fell in love with her. My time in the army ended in March 1960 and I prepared to fly home to the United States. I wanted to return to my life as a music star, but I was unhappy about leaving Priscilla and we promised to meet again soon.

♦ ◆ ♦

When I arrived home, I found that Colonel Parker had plans for me. I recorded my tenth album and we called it *Elvis is Back*, but he didn't want me to give many live performances. The Colonel thought we could earn more money from films, and filming took most of my time. I acted in 31 films altogether. But I wasn't very happy. The films were made too quickly, the songs were written too quickly and I missed singing real rock and roll to real people.

In 1962, Priscilla returned to the United States, and she soon came to live at Graceland. I was often in Hollywood making films, while Priscilla stayed in Memphis. In May 1967, I married Priscilla and nine months later, our daughter, Lisa Marie, was born. Our marriage lasted until 1973.

I loved earning huge amounts of money and meeting the President of the United States. But I was a simple boy from Tupelo and I found my celebrity life difficult. Reporters and photographers followed me everywhere. I developed addictions, and my health wasn't good. I tried to find meaning in my life, and I read many books, looking for answers.

After their big success, the British pop group, the Beatles, had found life difficult like me. They advised me to get help from spiritual leaders, but nothing worked for me. The happy times in my life had been long ago – singing gospel songs in church and playing on my first guitar.

I continued to suffer from depression. Colonel Parker arranged a tour for me, with the first concert in Rapid City, Cincinnati. My voice was still strong, but my body was weak. I died on 16th August 1977, aged just 42. I felt I had lived an amazing life, and people all over the world called me the King of Rock and Roll.

The Life of Elvis Presley

1935   Elvis Aaron Presley was born on 8th January in Tupelo, Mississippi, in the Deep South of the United States. His identical twin brother died.

1938   Vernon Presley, Elvis's father, was sent to prison for eight months. Elvis and his mother, Gladys, had to leave their home.

1946   Elvis received a guitar for his eleventh birthday.

1948   The Presley family moved to Memphis, Tennessee.

1950   A neighbour gave Elvis guitar lessons.

1953   Elvis left school and took a job as a truck driver.

1954   Elvis began to record songs for Sam Philips, who owned Sun Records, Memphis, performing with Scotty Moore and Bill Black. They recorded 'That's All Right Mama', which was played on the radio. Young people loved the new sound. They formed a band called the Blue Moon Boys.

1956   Colonel Tom Parker became Elvis's manager.
        He was sure that he could make Elvis into
        a star. Elvis recorded his famous song,
        'Heartbreak Hotel', in Nashville and appeared
        on television for the first time. Elvis signed his
        first contract with RCA Victor Records. His
        first album, *Elvis Presley*, was released and he
        performed several live shows. He acted in his
        first film, *Love Me Tender*.

1957   He was earning a lot of money, and bought
        Graceland Mansion in Mississippi. His third
        film, *Jailhouse Rock*, was a huge success.

1958   Film journalists liked his role in the film *King
        Creole*. Like many young Americans, Elvis had
        to join the US Army for two years, and he
        was sent to Germany. His mother fell ill, and
        he was allowed to return home to visit her.
        His mother's death sent him into a depression.
        He returned to Germany and met Priscilla
        Beaulieu when she came to a party at his
        house.

1960   He returned to the USA and began recording
        music again, releasing *Elvis is Back* and *GI
        Blues*. His fans were very happy that he was
        back in the USA.

1961   Elvis spent most of his time in Hollywood,
        acting in many films, including *Viva Las Vegas*
        and *Blue Hawaii*. Elvis performed a number of
        charity shows, but fewer live performances.

1965   The Beatles visited Elvis at his home in Bel Air, California.

1967   Elvis and Priscilla married at the Aladdin Hotel, Las Vegas. The next year, their daughter, Lisa Marie, was born in Memphis.

1969   Elvis performed 57 shows in one month at the International Hotel, Las Vegas.

1970   He met President Nixon at the White House in Washington, DC.

1973   Elvis and Priscilla ended their marriage. He began to suffer health problems.

1975   He won an award for 'How Great Thou Art'. He performed a New Year show in Michigan, receiving the largest amount of money for a single show by a single artist.

1976   He suffered badly from depression, and addictions. He had put on a lot of weight, and he looked terrible.

1977   He began his last concert tour in Rapid City, Cincinnati. He died aged 42, at Graceland in Memphis, Tennessee on 16th August.

acrobat COUNTABLE NOUN
An **acrobat** is a performer who does difficult physical acts such as jumping and balancing, especially in a circus.

addiction VARIABLE NOUN
An **addiction** is a situation in which you cannot stop yourself doing things such as taking drugs or drinking alcohol.

agent COUNTABLE NOUN
An **agent** is someone who finds work for performers such as actors and singers, and who takes care of their financial affairs.

ambitious ADJECTIVE
If you are **ambitious**, you want to be very successful at what you do. If you are **ambitious for** someone, you want them to be very successful.

audition TRANSITIVE VERB, INTRANSITIVE VERB
If someone **auditions**, or auditions **for** something, they give a short performance so that a director or conductor can decide if they are good enough to be in a play, film, or orchestra. You can also say that a director or conductor **auditions** someone.
COUNTABLE NOUN
An **audition** is a short performance that someone gives so that a director or conductor can decide if they are good enough to be in a play, film, or orchestra.

blues PLURAL NOUN
The blues is a type of music which is similar to jazz, with a slow tempo and a strong rhythm.

booking COUNTABLE NOUN
A **booking** is the arrangement that is made when a theatre agrees to have a performance by a singer or group of performers on a particular date.

boxer COUNTABLE NOUN
A **boxer** is someone who regularly takes part in the sport of boxing.

brass band COUNTABLE NOUN
A **brass band** is a musical band made up of metal instruments, such as trumpets, and instruments that you hit, such as drums.

celebrity COUNTABLE NOUN
A **celebrity** is a performer who is famous because he or she appears regularly on television, in films, or in newspapers and magazines.

cello VARIABLE NOUN
A **cello** is a musical instrument that looks like a large violin. You hold it upright and play it sitting down.

civil war COUNTABLE NOUN
A **civil war** is a war which is fought between different groups of people who live in the same country.

Cold War PROPER NOUN
The Cold War was the period after the Second World War when relations between the Soviet Union and the countries in the West were very difficult, and the two groups did not cooperate in any way.

colonel COUNTABLE NOUN, TITLE NOUN
A **colonel** is a senior officer in an army or air force. Sometimes, people use the title **Colonel** after they have left the military.

composition UNCOUNTABLE NOUN
Composition is the work of writing and arranging a piece of music, especially when this is done in accordance with music theory.

conductor COUNTABLE NOUN
A **conductor** is the person who stands in front of an orchestra or choir and directs its performance.

confident ADJECTIVE
People who are **confident** feel sure of their own abilities, qualities, or ideas and are not shy when they perform in public.

contract COUNTABLE NOUN
A **contract** is a legal agreement between people or companies. It usually involves one side agreeing to do some work or give a service and the other side agreeing to pay for the work or the service.

country music UNCOUNTABLE NOUN
Country music is a style of popular music from the southern United States.

crazy ADJECTIVE
If someone **goes crazy**, they start behaving in a wild and uncontrolled way.

dance hall COUNTABLE NOUN
Dance halls were large rooms or buildings where people used to pay to go and dance, usually in the evening.

debut COUNTABLE NOUN
When a performer **makes** his or her **debut**, he or she performs in public for the first time.

Deep South PROPER NOUN
The Deep South consists of the states that are furthest south in the United States.

democratic ADJECTIVE
A **democratic** country, organization, or system is governed by representatives who are elected by the people.

depressed ADJECTIVE
If you are **depressed**, you are sad and feel you cannot enjoy anything, because your situation is difficult and unpleasant.

depression UNCOUNTABLE NOUN
If someone has **depression**, they are very unhappy, have no energy, and find it difficult to do things.

devoted ADJECTIVE
If you are **devoted to** someone or something, you care about them or love them very much.

equal rights PLURAL NOUN
Equal rights are when everyone in society gets equal treatment and equal opportunities, whatever their race, sex, or religion.

free ADJECTIVE
1 If a country is **free**, it can govern itself and is not controlled by force or by a foreign country.

2 If you have **free** time, you are not working or busy and can do what you want to do.

French Foreign Legion
PROPER NOUN
The French Foreign Legion is a part of the French army that is made up of people from many different countries.

French Riviera PROPER NOUN
The French Riviera is the southeast area of France by the Mediterranean Sea.

gang COUNTABLE NOUN
A **gang** is a group of people who spend a lot of time together, often involved in crime or violence.

gangster COUNTABLE NOUN
A **gangster** is a member of a group of violent criminals.

glamorous ADJECTIVE
If you describe something as **glamorous**, you mean that it is more attractive, exciting, or interesting than ordinary things.

gospel UNCOUNTABLE NOUN
Gospel or **gospel music** is a style of religious music that uses

strong rhythms, and voices that sing different notes at the same time.

hip COUNTABLE NOUN
Your **hips** are the two areas or bones at the sides of your body between the tops of your legs and your waist.

impressed ADJECTIVE
If you are **impressed by** someone or something, you think they are very good and you admire them.

judge COUNTABLE NOUN
A **judge** is the person in a court of law who decides how the law should be applied, for example how criminals should be punished.

kidnap TRANSITIVE VERB
To **kidnap** someone is to take them away illegally and by force, and usually to hold them prisoner in order to demand something from their family, employer, or government.

maestro TITLE NOUN
Maestro is used as a title for a skilled and well-known musician or conductor.

masterclass COUNTABLE NOUN
A **masterclass** is a lesson where someone who is an expert at

something such as dancing or music gives advice to a group of good students. Masterclasses usually take place in public or are broadcast on television.

musical theatre VARIABLE NOUN
Musical theatre is a style of performance that combines singing, acting, and dancing.
COUNTABLE NOUN
A **musical theatre** is a theatre where there are regular performances of shows that involve singing, acting, and dancing.

nickname COUNTABLE NOUN
A **nickname** is an informal name for someone or something.

orchestra COUNTABLE NOUN
An **orchestra** is a large group of musicians who play a variety of different instruments together.

papa COUNTABLE NOUN
Some people refer to or address their father as **papa**.

prejudice VARIABLE NOUN
Prejudice against a person or group of people is an unreasonable dislike of them which leads to them being treated very badly or unfairly.

proud ADJECTIVE
1 If you feel **proud**, you feel pleasure and satisfaction at something that you have achieved.

2 Someone who is **proud** has a lot of dignity and self-respect.

3 Someone who is **proud** feels that they are better or more important than other people.

ragtime UNCOUNTABLE NOUN
Ragtime is a kind of jazz piano music that was invented in America in the early 1900s.

regret TRANSITIVE VERB
If you **regret** something that you have done, you wish that you had not done it.

release TRANSITIVE VERB
1 To **release** someone who has been held as a prisoner means to set them free.

2 When a performer or company **releases** a new record, video, or film, they make it available so that people can buy it or see it.

Resistance PROPER NOUN
The Resistance is a group of people who fight against the army that has invaded their country and now controls it.

risk COUNTABLE NOUN
If you **take** a **risk**, you do something that might have bad or unpleasant results.

rock and roll UNCOUNTABLE NOUN
Rock and roll is a kind of pop music developed in the 1950s which has a strong beat for dancing.

role COUNTABLE NOUN
A **role** is one of the characters that an actor or singer plays in a film, play, or opera.
COUNTABLE NOUN
Someone's **role** in a process or activity is their particular job in it.

ruins PHRASE
If a place or building is **in ruins**, it has been very badly damaged and almost completely destroyed.

scare COUNTABLE NOUN
A **scare** is a situation in which someone is afraid or worried because something dangerous is happening which might have a very bad result.

shack COUNTABLE NOUN
A **shack** is a small, simple hut built from bits of wood or metal.

shipping company
COUNTABLE NOUN
A **shipping company** is a company that owns a lot of ships and earns money by transporting goods in them.

shock TRANSITIVE VERB
If something **shocks** people, it upsets or offends them because they think it is rude or morally wrong.
COUNTABLE NOUN
If you have a **shock**, you suddenly have an unpleasant or surprising experience.

shocked ADJECTIVE
If you are **shocked**, you are suddenly and unpleasantly surprised by something bad.

show business
UNCOUNTABLE NOUN
Show business is the entertainment industry.

solo ADJECTIVE
A **solo** instrument or a **solo** performance involves only one person or instrument.
ADVERB
If a singer or other musician performs **solo**, they sing or play an instrument on their own rather than with a group of others.

soprano COUNTABLE NOUN
A **soprano** is a woman singer with a high voice.

soul UNCOUNTABLE NOUN
Soul or **soul music** is a type of pop music performed mainly by black American musicians.

sound COUNTABLE NOUN
You can use **sound** when you are describing what a style of music is like.

spiritual ADJECTIVE
Spiritual means relating to people's religious beliefs.

stammer INTRANSITIVE VERB
If someone **stammers**, they speak with difficulty, hesitating and repeating words or sounds.
COUNTABLE NOUN
If someone has a **stammer**, they speak with difficulty, hesitating and repeating words or sounds.

strain UNCOUNTABLE NOUN
Strain is pressure on a muscle or other part of your body that can cause damage.

street
on the streets PHRASE
If someone is **on the streets**, they do not have a home and have to sleep outside.

style UNCOUNTABLE NOUN
A **style** of music is a way of performing it that is associated with a particular place, performer, or musician.

COUNTABLE NOUN
Someone's **style of** doing something is the particular way they have of doing it.

superpower COUNTABLE NOUN
A **superpower** is a very powerful and influential country, usually one that has nuclear weapons and is economically successful.

talent VARIABLE NOUN
Talent is the natural ability to do something well.

talent show/competition
COUNTABLE NOUN
A **talent show** is a show where ordinary people perform an act on stage, usually in order to try to win a prize for the best performance.

tough ADJECTIVE
A **tough** area, period of time, or way of life is difficult , often because people have no money and there is a lot of crime and violence.

trumpet COUNTABLE NOUN
A **trumpet** is a metal musical instrument which you blow into.

violinist COUNTABLE NOUN
A **violinist** is someone who plays the violin.

waif COUNTABLE NOUN
If you refer to a child or young woman as a **waif**, you mean that they are very thin and look as if they have nowhere to live.

Wall Street Crash PROPER NOUN
The Wall Street Crash was an event that happened in 1929 in the USA when the value of the shares of a lot of companies fell a long way. This led to a depression that lasted 10 years, during which many companies stopped working and many workers lost their jobs.

Collins
English Readers

AMAZING PEOPLE READERS AT OTHER LEVELS:

Level 1

Amazing Inventors
978-0-00-754494-3

Amazing Leaders
978-0-00-754492-9

Amazing Entrepreneurs and Business People
978-0-00-754501-8

Amazing Women
978-0-00-754493-6

Amazing Performers
978-0-00-754508-7

Level 2

Amazing Aviators
978-0-00-754495-0

Amazing Architects and Artists
978-0-00-754496-7

Amazing Composers
978-0-00-754502-5

Amazing Mathematicians
978-0-00-754503-2

Amazing Medical People
978-0-00-754509-4

Level 4

Amazing Thinkers and Humanitarians
978-0-00-754499-8

Amazing Scientists
978-0-00-754500-1

Amazing Writers
978-0-00-754506-3

Amazing Leaders
978-0-00-754507-0

Amazing Entrepreneurs and Business People
978-0-00-754511-7

Visit **www.collinselt.com/readers** for language activities, teacher's notes, and to find out more about the series.